BEST IN SHOW

David Catrow

Orchard Books
An Imprint of Scholastic Inc.
New York

For Larry, Mo, and Squirrelly — D.C.

Text and illustrations copyright © 2011 by David Catrow

Library of Congress Cataloging-in-Publication Data
Catrow, David.
Max Spaniel : Best in Show / David Catrow. — 1st ed.
p. cm. — (Max Spaniel ; 3)
Summary: Max Spaniel outperforms all of the other entrants in a dog show.
ISBN 978-0-545-12277-1
[1. Dog shows—Fiction. 2. Spaniels—Fiction. 3. Dogs—Fiction. 4. Humorous stories.]
I. Title. II. Title: Best in Show.
PZ7.C2713Mav 2011 • [E]—dc22 • 2010047442

10 9 8 7 6 5 4 3 2 1   11 12 13 14 15
Printed in Singapore 46 • Reinforced Binding for Library Use • First edition, September 2011

The artwork was created using pencil sketches and Photoshop.
The display text was set in Good Girl.
The series display text was set in Mandingo.
The text was set in Old Style 1.
Book design by Whitney Lyle

My name is Max.
I am not a dog.

I am a famous star.

My cool cousin Spaniel L. Jackson
was a big star.

When I get dressed,
I have to look the part.

Wrong.

Wrong.

Awesome!

Today I am getting ready for the big show

I can act sad.　　　I can act mad.

I can act funny and wild!

There are many dogs in the show,

but there is only one me.

The show begins.

Spot hangs ten.
Fifi tries a swan dive.
Buster does a belly flop.
I dive —

for sunken treasure.

The barking contest begins.

Buster howls.
Fifi yips.
Spot woofs.

Anyone can bark like a dog

I quack like a duck

and roar like a lion.

It's time for the talent contes[t]

Fifi wears a hat.

Buster sits.

Spot shakes.

It is my turn, so I make shadow puppets

I'm pretty good at it.

The judge says,
"Let's start the music contest."

Spot starts to swing.
Buster plays the strings.
Fifi keeps the beat.
The judge taps his feet.

And I start to sing.

Buster, Fifi, and Spot bowwow.

And I just bow.

We all get a prize.

DAVID CATROW

is the creator of the Max Spaniel series: *Dinosaur Hunt, Funny Lunch,* and *Best in Show.* Max Spaniel is based upon David's dog Bubbs.

David Catrow lives with his wife, Debbie, and their dogs in Springfield, Ohio.

You can visit David at www.catrow.com.